T0142665

AuthorHouse™
1663 Liberty Drive
Bloomington, IN 47403
www.authorhouse.com
Phone: 833-262-8899

Because of the dynamic nature of the Internet, any web addresses or links contained in this book may have changed since publication and may no longer be valid. The views expressed in this work are solely those of the author and do not necessarily reflect the views of the publisher, and the publisher hereby disclaims any responsibility for them.

This book is printed on acid-free paper.

ISBN: 978-1-6655-4580-8 (sc)
ISBN: 978-1-6655-4579-2 (e)
ISBN: 978-1-6655-4578-5 (hc)

Library of Congress Control Number: 2021924078

Print information available on the last page.

Published by AuthorHouse 01/26/2022

authorHOUSE®

**To my dad and my sons,
I love you more than you know...**

To my father, John. I am forever grateful to you for helping instill a love of nature in my soul from the time I was a little girl. Thank you for giving me the most beautiful and special childhood.

To my teenage sons, Luke and Brayden. I have strived to show you as much nature as possible during your childhood, just like grandpa showed me (a tough act to follow). I will always treasure having been able to come to your middle school classrooms to teach you and your classmates about DNA, and to guide you through your very own hands on DNA isolation lab experiment. The look of pride, excitement, and empowerment on your faces was a moment I will cherish always.

Finally, this book is dedicated to the future SCIENTISTS waiting to emerge and do incredible things in the universe!

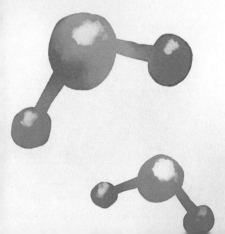

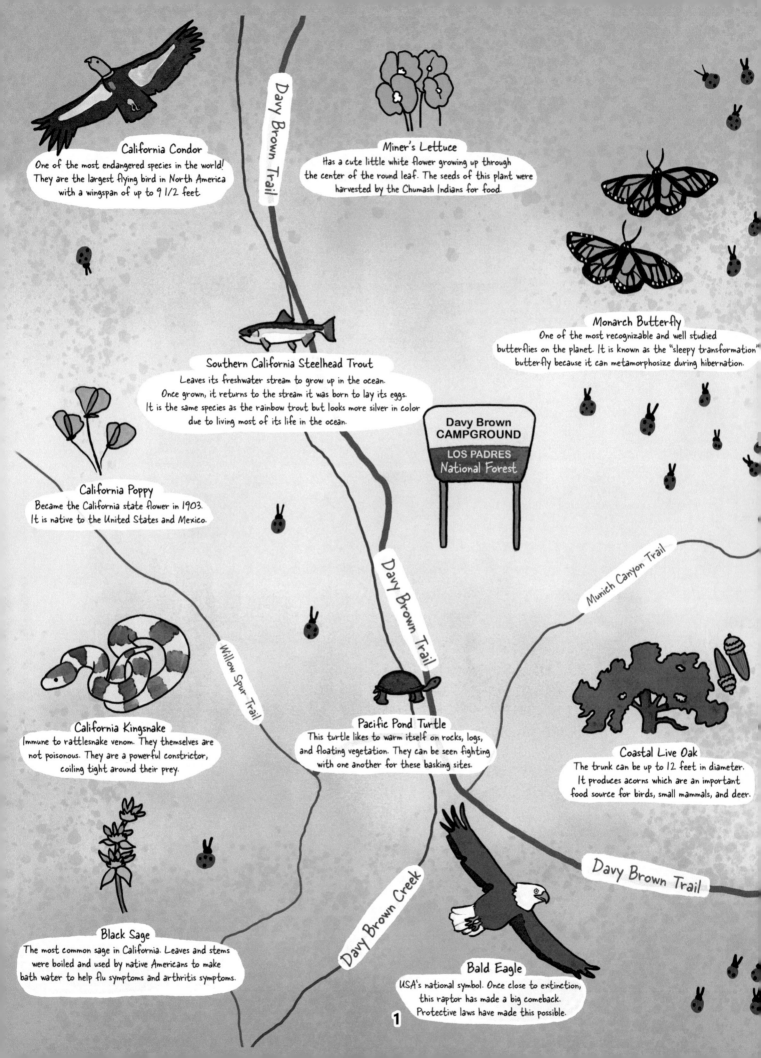

California Condor
One of the most endangered species in the world!
They are the largest flying bird in North America
with a wingspan of up to 9 1/2 feet.

Davy Brown Trail

Miner's Lettuce
Has a cute little white flower growing up through
the center of the round leaf. The seeds of this plant were
harvested by the Chumash Indians for food.

Monarch Butterfly
One of the most recognizable and well studied
butterflies on the planet. It is known as the "sleepy transformation"
butterfly because it can metamorphosize during hibernation.

Southern California Steelhead Trout
Leaves its freshwater stream to grow up in the ocean.
Once grown, it returns to the stream it was born to lay its eggs.
It is the same species as the rainbow trout but looks more silver in color
due to living most of its life in the ocean.

Davy Brown
CAMPGROUND
LOS PADRES
National Forest

California Poppy
Became the California state flower in 1903.
It is native to the United States and Mexico.

Munich Canyon Trail

Davy Brown Trail

Willow Spur Trail

California Kingsnake
Immune to rattlesnake venom. They themselves are
not poisonous. They are a powerful constrictor,
coiling tight around their prey.

Pacific Pond Turtle
This turtle likes to warm itself on rocks, logs,
and floating vegetation. They can be seen fighting
with one another for these basking sites.

Coastal Live Oak
The trunk can be up to 12 feet in diameter.
It produces acorns which are an important
food source for birds, small mammals, and deer.

Davy Brown Trail

Davy Brown Creek

Black Sage
The most common sage in California. Leaves and stems
were boiled and used by native Americans to make
bath water to help flu symptoms and arthritis symptoms.

Bald Eagle
USA's national symbol. Once close to extinction,
this raptor has made a big comeback.
Protective laws have made this possible.

There once was a girl who loved nature and the great outdoors. She often went on amazing adventures like backpacking with her dad. She felt happy being outdoors.

After a long day of hiking trails, the adventurous pair dozed off under a blanket of stars. They watched satellites cross the great galaxies. She thought of the fun backpacking day she had with her dad.

Satellites

Satellites can travel at 18,000 miles per hour! They can travel the entire circumference of the Earth about 14 times in a day.

Her belly was full of delicious trout they caught, and Miner's Lettuce salad they harvested from the forest. She thought of the tasty Jello dessert they made by using the cold creek as a "refrigerator".

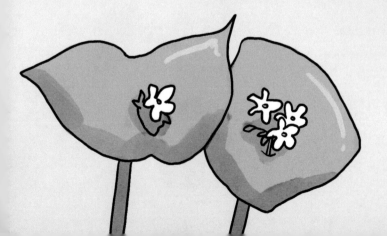

Heads Up!

Never eat wild plants unless your parent is trained in botany (the scientific study of plants) and says it is okay to do so.

Back home from the wilderness in her own cozy bed, she wondered what her next adventure might be. She reflected on favorite memories so far in her young life. She didn't yet realize they were all SCIENCE! She fell deep into a wonderful dream...

With a lab coat dressed SCIENCE fairy as her guide, the adventure began...

" You will have a quirky chemistry teacher who makes chemistry fun! He will make it easy to learn the subject. He will help you realize that you want to learn more about SCIENCE!

Atoms, Valence Electrons, & Orbitals

An atom is the smallest unit of matter that forms a chemical element.

Atoms are made up of three particles: protons, neutrons, and electrons.

Valence electrons are negatively charged particles in the outer most shell of an atom.

Orbitals are areas within atoms where there is a high chance of finding electrons.

You will study Biological Sciences at Cal Poly San Luis Obispo. You will love that Cal Poly is a hiking friendly college town! Your childhood hiking passion will reignite as you hike for fun with your computer SCIENCE roommate and best friend between your studies.

You won't know how lucky you are to live steps from the ocean in Avila Beach during your last year at Cal Poly! You will study on the beach and you will enjoy beautiful runs along the coast while you reflect on the SCIENCE you learned in your classes each day.

San Luis Yacht Club

AVILA BEACH

Photosynthesis
Photosynthesis
Photosynthesis

Cal Poly
Research
Pier

Photosynthesis

$$6CO_2 + 6H_2O + \downarrow$$
$$C_6H_{12}O_6 + 6O_2$$

What is Photosynthesis?

Photosynthesis produces most of Earth's oxygen. 50-70% of this oxygen comes from ocean plants!

Olde Port Inn

FATCATS cafe

You will discover triathlon, the fun sport of "swim, bike, run"! You will do your first race just for fun while attending Cal Poly! This will come back to you many years later as a life passion!

Kinesiology

The scientific study of human body movement, including:
- Physiological
- Biomechanical
- Anatomical
- Neuropsychological

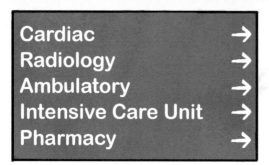

Cardiac →
Radiology →
Ambulatory →
Intensive Care Unit →
Pharmacy →

PHARMACY

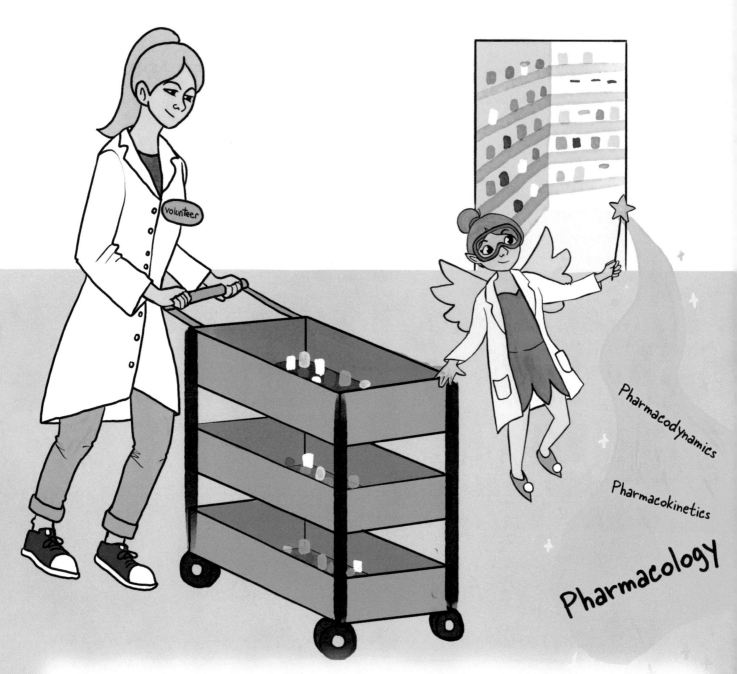

Pharmacodynamics

Pharmacokinetics

Pharmacology

You will love learning about SCIENCE so much that you will take extra college chemistry classes just for fun! These extra classes will inspire you to volunteer in the pharmacy at a local San Luis Obispo hospital between classes.

Your first job will be at the famous, historical Caltech (California Institute of Technology, Pasadena, California)! You will make biochemicals for post-doctoral student research! Your coworkers and student "customers" will be from all over the world!

Biopolymer Synthesis Lab

Peptide: A short chain of amino acids (2–50).

Protein: A longer chain of amino acids (more than 50).

Tyr
(Tyrosine)

Ala
(Alanine)

Cys
(Cysteine)

Ile
(Isoleucine)

Val
(Valine)

Pro
(Proline)

Gly
(Glycine)

Peptides are important to our biological health. Our bodies make them and they can be made by pharmaceutical companies for use in medicines.

Steps of Peptide Synthesis

Deprotect

Neutralize

Couple

Cap

Vitamin C

$C_6H_8O_6$

Vitamin C

$C_6H_8O_6$

$C_6H_8O_6$

Linus Pauling
Celebration of Life

Beckman Auditorium,
Caltech
Nov. 18, 1994

California Institute of Technolog

While working at Caltech, you will attend two very special celebrations in honor of two world famous SCIENTISTS who attended Caltech as students!

Linus Pauling, was an American chemist, biochemist, chemical engineer, peace activist, author, and educator. He received two Nobel Prizes, each in separate fields. His discoveries inspired the work of SCIENTISTS like Watson and Crick on the structure of DNA. This made it possible for SCIENTISTS to crack the DNA code for all organisms. He also had an interest in Vitamin C and did a lot of research on this molecule.

Edward Lewis was an American geneticist and a co-recipient of a Nobel Prize in Physiology or Medicine for his fruit fly research. He helped found the field of evolutionary developmental biology.

Fruit Fly

Fruit fly (Drosophila Melanogaster) genetic studies have helped scientists to understand diseases in humans.

C'mon, let's go check out the world of industry!

**Edward Lewis
Caltech campus
Nobel Prize celebration
1995**

You will work for many years at one of the largest medical testing labs in the world! There, you will become a R&D (Research and Development) SCIENTIST. You will develop many products to help people be healthier. One of these products will be a test to help diagnose human growth disorders! Together, you and your colleagues will earn a United States patent for your company for work related to this.

U.S. Patent

A U.S. patent is a right given to an inventor that prevents others from making, selling, or using the invention for a period of time.

This job will take you to Boston University to train a famous Vitamin D SCIENTIST'S post-doctoral research students how to run a Vitamin D medical test that you helped to develop!

You will forever treasure your career as a R&D SCIENTIST, but you'll be ready for your next SCIENCE adventure!

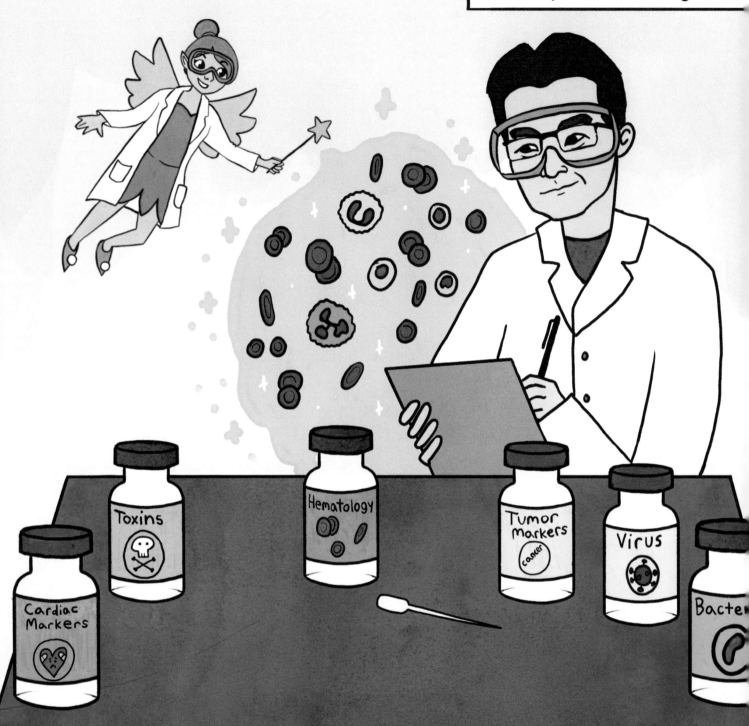

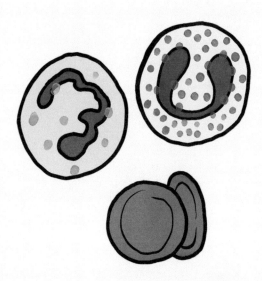

You will lead teams to develop medical device products and bring them to market! You will learn the big picture of business while still keeping SCIENCE close to your heart! The projects you will manage will produce products that help make sure the medical tests of the world are working properly! These products will help diagnose many people's health issues.

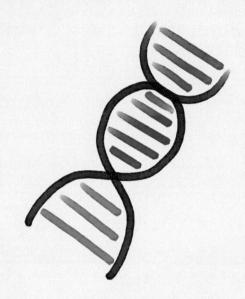

This medical device company will value teaching children about SCIENCE. You will participate in their wonderful program to help inspire kids to love SCIENCE. You will visit students' classrooms and lead them in a hands on lab to collect, extract, and isolate their own DNA to wear home in a necklace! More than two thousand of your own children's schoolmates will be given this special opportunity to consider becoming SCIENTISTS when they grow up! They will love being able to actually see their precipitated DNA in their necklaces.

Precipitation

The creation of a solid from a solution. The solid formed from a reaction in liquid solution is called a "precipitant".

You will become "Principal for a Day" at your own kids middle school! You will get to talk to the AVID kids about your journey in SCIENCE!

A world pandemic will hit and you will be tasked with the project of your lifetime. You will lead a team to develop products to help fight COVID-19!

Your career will flash before your eyes as a gift that you suddenly know you must share with children. You will have so much fun writing a children's book to share your SCIENCE journey with kids! "

"The important thing is to never stop questioning."

-Albert Einstein

"Nothing in life is to be feared, it is only to be understood."

-Marie Curie

"Somewhere, something incredible is waiting to be known."

-Carl Sagan

"Education is the most powerful weapon which you can use to change the world."

-Nelson Mandela

About the Illustrator

Hanna Smith is a graphic designer and illustrator born and raised in Orange County California. Ever since she was young, she's always loved to draw. She is studying graphic design and illustration at Laguna College of Art and Design and will graduate in May 2022. This project was her first time illustrating a children's book, and she loved the experience. Ultimately, she hopes to bring positivity and happiness with her wherever she goes.

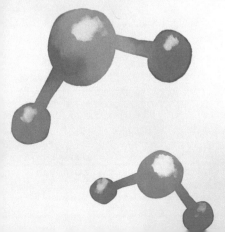

Printed in the United States
by Baker & Taylor Publisher Services